HIPology: Horizons In Poetry

HIPology

Edited by
Ron Allen and Stella L. Crews

BROADSIDE PRESS
P.O. BOX 04257
Detroit, MI 48204

For
Dudley Randall

Pictured above are John Mason, Wardell Montgomery Jr., and Ron Allen, founders of HIP (Horizons In Poetry), a reading series which began in 1982. First housed at Cobb's Corner, a jazz bar in the Cass Corridor, it moved, in 1985, to Alexander's, its present location at Woodward Avenue and Canfield. Every second Tuesday of the month a featured reader is followed by an open- mike performance which begins at 8 PM. This literary endeavor continues with the able assistance of Sharon Smith-Knight and Trinidad Sanchez, Jr. Sixty-five of the seventy five poets who have been featured readers for Horizons In Poetry are presented here, forever bound to each other.

ACKNOWLEDGMENTS

The editors and publisher extend special thanks
to the following persons:

Joe Vicari of Alexander's Lounge, Michele Gibbs for the
cover art, George Lee for the cover design, Willie Williams for
the photo of HIP's founders, Leisia Duskin for the layout,
Geoffrey Jacques for the title of this anthology and
Joann Cox for typesetting.

CONTENTS

Satchmo: Man About to Die   15   In Detroit Meadows   16
Black Socrates   18
    Ray McKinney
Consolation   19
    Clear Land
Open the Sky For Air   20
    M.L. Liebler
On Going to Kill Deer and Finding Them Uncooperative   21
    Rick McKenzie
Untitled   23
    Leslie Reese
Enticement   24
    Philip Royster

The Artist   25
    John Mason
Jump   27
    Wardell Montgomery, Jr.
Snowfire   28
    Errol A. Henderson
In My Addiction I Study Foucault   30   In Tampere   31
    Sadiq Bey
Words & Music in America   32   Late Summer 1988   33
For John Coltrane   34
    Kofi Natambu
Chewing Gum   35   Wine Sip   37
    Sharon Smith-Knight
Lycia   38
    Dave Lee

Tiananmen Square   39   For Wild Women   41
    Marie Stephens
Guns Really Don't Kill People   43   New Year Resolution   44
    Alvin Aubert
From Hunger   45
    Geoffrey Jacques
Dream Number I   48   Am I Who   49
    Ron Allen

The Musician   51   Hope   52   Azania   53
   Michael Nance
The Deep Hat Boys   54
   Faruq Z. Bey
Zelime   56
   Sybil Kein
Untitled I   57   Untitled II   59
   Kim Hunter
After Mechanic Tuned the Engine, It Ran Out of Key   61
Untitled I   62   Untitled II   63
   Teresa Tan
Driving Through the Fog   64
   José L. Garza

Hackensack   66
   John Sinclair
Passatempo   70
   Paul F. Lichter
Images   71
   Naomi Long Madgett
South Africa Lives Here   72   Revolution is Realism   75
   Nubia Kai
The Crystal Globe I   77
   Hernan Castellano-Giron
Summer   78   Snoring   79
   Lawrence Pike
Hamp and Marie   81
   Carolyn Burke
From: Thiz Singular Voice I, II, III   82
   Ibn Pori Pitts

A Remembered Candle   84   The River   85
Winterblood   86
   Rod Reinhart
Penman's Song   87
   Angeline Kaimala
Indian Summer   88   Beats   89
   MaryAnn Cameron
The Vesper of Vietman   90
   Melba Boyd

Scenario in a Check Out Lane 92   Name Poem I 94
    Saundra Douglas
Snow Corn 96   For Tina Turner 98
    Leisia Duskin
Standoff 99
    Larry Gabriel
Cafe au Lait 100   Nocturnal Emissions 102
    Keith Sterling
Desire and Free Trade 103
    Charles Gervin
Queen of the Molar Derby 104   Rigor of Mortise 105
    Dennis Teichman

Peace for Ali Muhammad 107
    Kaleema Hasan
Tenor Tears 108
    Willie Williams
Making Hate 110
    Irv Barat
Private Fire 111   Passion Fruit 112
    Steve Schreiner
No. 125: Incident at the Tea Party 113
    Rico Africa
Why Do Men Wear Earrings on One Ear? 114
Chicano Warriors 115
    Trinidad Sanchez, Jr.
#56 117
    Rob Rudnick

Collard Green Fields Forever 118   Calling All Brothers 119
    Aneb Kgositsile
Untitled 122
    Kim Nolte-Avalon
Trash & Shout 123
The Day We Threw Out the Xmas Tree 124
    Chris Tysh
Rutha Jean: White Friend of My Childhood 125
    Hilda Vest
On a Hunger Strike 126
    Mick Vranich
Untitled 127
    Ruby Woods

Wild Kingdom   128   A Good Left Jab   129
A Black Man Who Wants to Be a White Woman   130
    Tyrone Williams
The Plagues   131   Die Cut   134
    Roberto Warren
Doors of Perception   135
    Allen Adkins
My Name   136
If You Don't Want My Love Poem   138
    Mildred Hunt

Love Poem #2   139
    Lolita Hernandez
Mike and Robin Must Love Each Other   141
Do You Know What It Means to Miss Detroit?   142
    Ray Waller
The Mouth of the River of Eyes   144
    Jahra Michelle McKinney
5   145
    David M. Glicker
From Reminder on the Wind   146
    Stella Crews
Religious Instructions: Book of Revelations 148   Laid Off 149
    Michele Gibbs
Sankai Juku: Butoh Dancers of the Soul   151
Memories of Mei   152
    Schaarazetta Natalege

Satchmo: Man About to Die

Wine drenched love
purpled their vision
tenderness. . . trembling,
touched the hurt where life begins . . .
and a baby sang some blues
hunkered down.
then sprang the tiny mouth
crying dark to hunger stingy life . . .
no hand to reach his need . . .
orphaned on a frozen stoop . . .
crysinging his song in a holler
the now child trumpeted . . .
gusting black . . .
ring tossed his mark . . .
came circling, blue,
ringing blue worlds!
lost mama who abandoned her child to means . . .
how sweet the fears that nurture.
where, father, the rough that challenges the face to sense?
but oh, the empty horn is filling,
that nurtured the blues . . .
that centered rings . . .
that emptied the horn . . .
that filled his life.
proud manchild blown from the King!
those fancies lit the cars that heard the ring
        of 20's polished brass!
that hankered brow showed its dark lit image bright as jazz . . .
just like purple love wine trembling in brass.
drink from that bright chalice children of frost.
sing to your mamas
tunes of a new age papa
goin' home to saints!

                    Ray McKinney

In Detroit Meadows

still burning after all these years,
in Detroit meadows,
an old one digs in his bag.
a burnt out crust of a man/ creature/ refugee,
a luckless cinder from the exhausted
    forges of Rouge.

It never did trickle down enough to cool
    him off.
I can tell by the draining abscesses he airs.
his disgusting disregard of rules,
trespasses our decencies
to burn us in our guts,
to blacken us in the anti-socialness of
    his fragrance.
wild flowers bloom on Eastern Market's
    square.

we missed again.
the space between the marks have grown
    between us
a stage. . .
whereon outrage and terror are play to
    the same old blues in the dark,
the random fires flower and illumines
    future's desperate face
in search of a suitable demise in
    resolution of our causes
a tomato rots in vain of a hungry bum.
never a return to faith,
or compost bursting of life after death,
fungi mushroom, ... spewing toxic spores
    in clouds that issue from his
    stillborn dreams.

the meadow is a triumph of failures
an overgrazed stoney desert in triumph
    after a rain..
. . . burst in fields of carrion flowers
    with their false meats
and dark centers exploding in
    untrammeled growth.
hump junky! honky jump!
through broken glass and bitter root.
    us burn the blazes of the dis possessed.

                                    Ray McKinney

17

Black Socrates

what senates judge my history
in dialogue veiled in anonymity?
with fiery crosses they build my fences,
I bemoan the past that jails my senses
while others harness magic,
I am steeped in antiquity so tragic.
and from the distant heaven's light
distant stars in silver columns
swimming bright,
shine through bars.
so..once again
I lift my hemlock cup
to sip away the meager rights
that trip and atrophy my heart.
while panic and alarm like wolves
that tear my bleating flock apart,
does me harm.
can still I see my image blameless?
I gasp the putrid air
to face the nameless fear aware that
     I tread the stingy measured steps
to my sojourns righteous end..
and dread the thoughts I ruminate,
while I wait and wait and wait and
wait . . . .

                         Ray McKinney

Consolation

The way you turn the cloth over
Your cupped fingers, that's the way
She yanked a tangled hank of hair,
Examining minutely
Each small fleck of green
In the small boy's eyes.
The pupils seemed to swell, the cool
Green irises to rain.
Unexpected,
This intense reaction!
Unexpected,
This silent, steady pain!
His small head, outraged,
Crumples
Onto his small pale chest.
Her brown fingers
Release their hold.
He sinks onto the mat, naked,
Among the rubber ducks, the frog,
And cries.
She stands beside the sink
And watches. Hands on her hips.
Her brown eyes cold.
He wipes his face with small pale hands.
She offers
No consolation, not a towel.
He rubs his head. He's going to tell
His mother.
That's all right. He'll never
Call nobody else
A nigger!

Clear Land

19

Open The Sky For Air
(for Faruq Z. Bey)

Crack it
Open. Widen the sky.
Let us stretch our necks
Through the hole created
To breathe in colors
That we can cultivate in our souls
And later make into words,
A love as bright as the stars
In the spectral night
Of rhythmical light.

Turn us on.
Make us believe
That color is a language
And that shadows can
Be brought to life
To dance us out
of our solitude and darkness,
And into a world
Where the dawn is a metaphor
Written by the sun.

M.L. Liebler

On Going to Kill Deer and Finding Them Uncooperative
(Homage to Li Po)

Somewhere, space aliens are cloning Elvis' brain.
Somewhere, housewives are losing weight a new way.
Somewhere, celebrities are getting remarried.

But I'm in the cedar swamp,
in its ultra-elaborate decor,
droplets of my breath swirling in the sunlight.

Somewhere, the board of directors is meeting.
Starting a national chain of blow-job crack houses,
The Thirteenth Nightmare On Your Street Part Nine.
They have just received big financial backing,
from major investment capital firms.
Their lawyers are busy.

But I'm sneaking. Walking so slow,
that the squirrels don't care.
Three different woodpeckers are jamming.
Wintergreen perfuming my steps,
club mosses losing their spores.

Somewhere, preachers are preaching against me.
The deadline for final submissions has past.
On T.V. there are lots of tight, shiny dresses.

But I'm standing still.
A while ago, I forgot to keep sneaking.
The mosses are hundreds of greens and grays.
From my left and behind me,
come a crack and a thump.
Three deer, in a line, go stampeding past me,
heads down, necks straight out,
running in long, flat, 20-foot leaps,

hooves pounding. Nothing could travel so fast.
I can't tell if there're antlers. A shot would be stupid.
Anyway I don't think a bullet could catch them.
My mouth is wide open. I sit down on a log.

Somewhere, there is a big opportunity.

But I'm in the cedar swamp, sitting.
I see thinning of dawns, the thickening twilight.
The deer brought me here,
their beauty, elusiveness, meat.
I'm so glad that I came.
I'm having a great time. Wish you were here.

Rick McKenzie

Untitled

I see my sisters on city buses, eating apples.
yellowjackets chase after the fire smell
    crushed yellow and pink in their palms.
and on a sunburst day
I hear them singing to the skies in the
    round of their bellies.

I see them wearing their hard brown
    fingernails shaped
and colored
by blood and afterbirths; cornmeal,
    ammonia, and the juice of
    themselves in love.

I see photographs of my hungry sisters
naked and crisp-boned against
a sea-green desert canvas
O
the silence.

I see them in autumn's ruby leaves:
    soft on the wind. dull on
    the pavement.
and some I see: bejewelled and moneyfingertipped
ashamed of their own laughter . . .
O
to peek
between the strands
of their beautiful hair.

Leslie A. Reese

Enticement

The evening sun's
luminous curved
bright platinum
bottom
hangs
just below
the slate hem
of clouds.

Philip Royster

The Artist

'Ere's an ole black fellow
'Is teeth are yellow
An' there's a knowing in his laugh

'E thinks thought mellow
Always says 'Ello
T' the folk who walk the path
O' the city streets
Where the 'ookers meet
Wi' the fellas wastin' gas

'E knows all the artists
'N the tinkering fartists
In 'is nutsy neighborhood

'E loves all the dogs
'n 'E sleeps like a log
When the weather turn to good

'E smiles and forms
thoughts soft and warm
T' the lowest and the meanest folk

'Is twinkle teases
'Is manner pleases
As 'E shows us all the joke

The place of decay
'E quickly relays
Into a magic glade

'E ambles along
Asingin' 'is song
Unfouled by gun or blade

An 'E makes it so easy
to see life as breezy
While living in the shade

Of crumbling culture
'Is life is a sculpture
That 'E as an artist, has made . . .

John Mason

Jump

He stood on the ledge of a 30
    story building
And said that he wanted to jump
I begged and pleaded with him not to
And told him life, though tough,
    is worth living

He spoke of children he abused
Women he raped and men he shot
I said let's talk about it
Let's try to work these feelings out
There must be hope for you

He said that he has been to a
    1,000 sessions
And that he still feels the same
Then he said he was the one who
    convinced my girlfriend
To take my money and my new car and
    run off with him

I said JUMP!

                Wardell Montgomery, Jr.

Snowfire

I.
55 gallon drums burst forth flames
like the fires of hell to warm chilled
bellies of the travelling bag entourage
down some another street
and from winterized cars and winterized homes
cold stares of passersby freeze the
        image in their minds
and icily remark
"Why don't they just go away"

II.
burning open cans flame in the cold
heat for some depressed soles
walking past up and down streets in
the city where once begging to strangers
for nickels and dimes has now become
quarters and dollars - the cost of living
        is going up
but the cost of dying runs about the same
and bagladys and bagmen will build snowfires
in garbage cans to stave off the frigid
        chill of winter
and coldhearted people

III.
he wants to lay his body down
before he dies
you ever see a bagman fall?
in the snow?
ever?
they don't get up

they don't do no dancing
they lie there and die there in the
      cold snowfire
chilled by death
with their warm blood's last pulsing
they die
just like they was human

Errol A. Henderson

From In My Addiction I Study Foucault

2.
we see the backs
of heads of those
gone before us. what
were they really looking for?
bags of tools, books of rules.
we anticipate
the exposure of bone and blood.
we are telekinetic seeking
the source of authorship.
doo wop doo wow.
because of the odd meter,
the motion of the feet
is disjointed, unpasteurized.
there are no holidays for
poets. in a moment's
notice we are supplanted
by the anchorperson, tube tied.
the cardigan replaces the
waist coat. a play on words.
it seems we've become a floppy disc.
our message in the crossword.
a jingle for used cars.
tomorrow, my book will be
on video cassette, there will
be nothing to sign at the party.

Sadiq Bey

In Tampere

there was nothing checkered
in tampere. no floors, no flags.
david murray jumped out
of a mirror made of diamonds.
the bass clarinet was a snake
hanging from his head. hotel lives
will never be the same.
steve and fred made the floor
shift without warning. the ballroom
was spellbound by the dark
sparkle of legerdemain. three
wrestling magicians dancing with
squirming equations.

2)
outside of the sphere,
another cage, leroy jenkins
helped us to levitate. we left
the luggage in the seats. what
weapons, his songs, what
formulas of purpose. the ferociousness
of silence magnified. we saw the eye
in the witchdoctor's hand and
began to float. we saw the marriage
of celestia and terrestria, a scene
that could not be seen.

Sadiq Bey

Words & Music in America

Jazz poetry was not discovered by
Allen Ginsberg or Jack Kerouac
let alone Kenny Rexroth
Nor was it a literary invention of the
Beat (up) school, the New York School or
any other official institution of 20th
century AVANT-learning
       It started if you really wanna know
       (and you damn well should) in a white
       whorehouse in East St. Louis, Illinois
       in August 1928 where a bunch of drunken
       unemployed Negro poets were sitting around
       trying to sound like LOUIS ARMSTRONG as a
       rickety Victrola ground out 1900 choruses
of "Tight Like That" in the early mourning
hours of Eddie Jefferson's 12th birthday
It was Eddie's father who told the other cats
present that they should all donate their individual
stanzas to little Eddie as a birthday gift as Jefferson, Sr.
didn't have no money as usual to buy his wideyed son that
silver-grey saxophone he'd seen in the window of a weary
looking pawnshop called LIGHTS OUT in the "nigger section"
of town
       The rest as they say is MYSTERY . . .

                Kofi Natambu

Late Summer 1988
(Brooklyn)

I can see the Statue
of Liberty from my rooftop
it's green & brown or is
that a dying sparrow spinning
crazily across the off-white horizon?
Drone & sigh cuts thru the twilight air
as I fitfully search for signs of VITALITY.

Down below various Tony Montanas are fighting
for miniscule territories that have not already
been claimed by Donald Trump.
Too many men from every nationality are
        aching
for a fight they have no intention of winning &
too many women are waiting ENDLESSLY for
        someone
to tell them how "pretty & interesting" they are.

Meanwhile a crackdealer asks me if I wanna cop
"How did you get way up here?" I ask him . . .

                              Kofi Natambu

For John Coltrane

Coltrane subdivides the air in
to massive columns of Space
He fills all the Space all the
Time with brazen mathematical emotions
Firestorms of disciplined thoughts
burn down the paths of certainty
A roaring expansion into millions of singing
labyrinths thundering toward the precise
articulation of what he knows & does not
No   All the Time in all the Space

              A face exploding into trillions of sounds
              A heart mowing down memories
              A soul sucking up the light   soaking the bones
              in Oceans of Energy   Air charging molecules
              inside holograms of Awareness
                      Intervals smashing stars and spitting them
                      out into the empty black sky

                      Coltrane is a terrible cleansing force
                      A holy divebomber in saxaphone Jets
                      A killer with the Healing eye
                      A Melodic arsonist
                      A Harmonic hieroglyph
                      A rhythmic hurricane
              Flowers that bleed
              real tears

                      Kofi Natambu

34

Chewing Gum

What happens to chewing gum
After all the sweetness is gone?

Some people continue to chew
Recalling absent flavors.

Others play it off
by blowing bubbles
or popping it loudly
as if punishing the gum
for its current blandness.

Many hold it hostage
on bedposts, behind ears
under chairs, or on refrigerator
shelves.

The more analytical
attempt to pinpoint
the precise moment
they realized the sugar was going.

I, on the other hand,
recognize a tasteless situation
when I see one.

I don't develop an emotional attachment,
I dispose of it quickly, in the wrapper provided,

I toss the crumpled mass
and go on with my life,
with no regrets!

Chewing gum is a lot like a stale relationship.

Isn't it comforting to know
that you can always get
a fresh piece?

Sharon Smith-Knight

Wine Sip

If you were a vintage bottle of wine
and I could fill my cup
I'd savor your essence for a time,
then slowly I'd drink you up.

I'd let you linger on my tongue
delight my palate with your bouquet
my lips would bathe in your crimson pool,
and I'd sit and sip all day.

If you were a bottle of vintage wine
all mellow and aged in wood
I'd whirl you and swirl you
around my mouth,
and hold you as long as I could.

I'd drink from you slowly and deeply,
and make your flavor last,
and I wouldn't stop
'till the very last drop,
and I'd probably lick my glass.

Sharon Smith-Knight

Lycia

I stand on a small cliff
Below a large whale gasps
Barely nudged by the surf
His long slick body heaves

Peering into his large lung
Full of the dying sea
I'm ready to commit him to negative
But fear and embarrassment arrange me

I refrain
Having offended the passing of life
And its theater of vehicles
Too much of late!

But still I want to shoot
All the gasping chambers
I want to know
        was he hunted
        does he bleed
        or is it suicide?

But then he is gone
And only night astounds
Lighting the tips of waves
As I listen to the music of pebbles

                      Dave Lee

Tiananmen Square

The dawn is grey, the misting light is moved by breezes
Painting patterns on these streets
So empty now
A soldier stands, within his hands the gun
Commands
A silence, and I hide my eyes.

But recognize, his face so barren
Of the smiles we shared just yesterday
As I lay
Upon the ground among the sleeping bodies
Of my lover and our friends
In Tiananmen Square.

You strangers/soldiers laughed and teased us
In your tongue
We thought that we had won
Defiance in the streets, our songs creating
Banners of the new in noise
The village coiled around us like a snake
Repulsed the tanks with empty-handed courage
Only
We could not understand, there had been a plan.

Suddenly, the shots cut through the waiting
Your gun became a revelation
And in the screaming, and in the slaughter
I saw the power that pulled the trigger
And pitted me against you in the pattern
of the State.

Stunned
The spreading crimson butterfly beneath my

hand
The reddened river running men and women
Wailing, cut between us in confusion
And I was swept away,
And I was swept away.

Marie Stephens

For Wild Women

When I was a wild woman
I checked my face in the mirror
Concentrated on my bit in the revolution
Set up my week-ends like a roadmap
Where were the blues?

I was hungry, wanting more
Rummaging through empty rapture
Raiding everyone

Faces, thighs
Pressing the flesh
On my campaign
I'd remember names
In momentary lapses.

Catching the gossip flak
Shrapnel
Waking up in stranger's places
Taxis home
Back in my kitchen by
Noon.

Drugs that shot me
Past my expectations
Riding that train down
Coltrane and a demon whistle
Blowing on my entrance or my exit.

Oh yes, Mr. Joyce
I made it past the net
Ran it out of bounds or at
Least closer to the forest's edge.

Premonitions of an ending
winded with a tired heart
As the thin veneer of "civilized" began to
Stiffen up my "loose".

So I'm singing this for you, wild women
Wild women don't get the blues
You learn that later

Marie Stephens

Guns Really Don't Kill People

they really don't, mama, people do
the young son reassures the mother
of the lost son his older brother
shot dead the first deer season day.

the disconsolate mother dutifully, stoically accepting the
sentence prepared for her by the NRA adding desperate
words of her own:

hunting's got to go on
the boys and men have just got to be more careful
that's all, she says to the brave young hunters
standing by so tall, under the spirited cameraed eye
of her only surviving son who beams approvingly,
eager to field test his new-bought hunting gun.

Alvin Aubert

New Year Resolution, 1990

You never put it down exactly the way
you saw it done or heard it said Americans
only speak God's English they don't write it
want to come to this country gotta talk
like God but even that's getting to be a thing
of the past says the black american business man
being interviewed on the tube who's trying
to figure out what his blackness means in the
business world whose business world?
he can't hear the question says *the* business
world if it's *the* business world how come
he's not in business oh miss minnie lee says from
her front porch it's a mess a real bloody
(she heard that on tv) mess like spell casting
like that man with the beeper over there that
young man with the beeper over there that young
blackamericanman with the beeper over there
the greatamerican unachievable predication steps
out of miss minnie lee's house onto her front porch
another young blackamericanman with a devil's night
smoke ring surrounding his heart every dumpster
in the city's on fire only the rats are disturbed
the tv man with the inconspicuous ultracompact
videocamera over there with the pomegranite bow tie
bluejay on his shoulder the radio offering for sale
chiseled off chunks of the Berlin Wall
the blackamerican businessman wonders if he can get
a piece of that too late to get into chisels.

Alvin Aubert

From Hunger

inside streets littered with burning teeth
streets where mutilated heads sway in the wind
— would the lock unfasten if I brought you a head on a pole
if I appeared as a genuine savage
the face in just the right pose

come to the back yard when a winter wind sweeps
        these stark
naked branches & see her frozen fast against a chain link
        fence
while inside young virgins howl over cold porridge

the pose is perfect
eyes bulging from their sockets
teeth white skin dark dark way too dark
there couldn't possibly be any virtue
hurry up with that pole. . .

. . . none of these shelters can shield a child
bombs hidden under sullen houses of garbage
hope drowned while the plate glass beacons from the far
    beyond
of our giddiness & the drama of a final hour hidden under
the flaky crust of a morning pleasantly surrounded

presumably that is genuine leather which protects you from
the opposite image which by its existence is proof positive of
your superiority flaky even as you admit it to be

there is a moral here to be sure
it's not your fault after all his weapons alone place him
beyond the pale dark dark way too dark. . .

. . . at the nadir of assumption: choices
open the door to hope
exchange the garbage for a hyena
reach up & turn on the lights
release our music from its presumed obligation to giddiness
ressurect in our atrophied memories the meaning
    of the clenched fist
of a screaming senseless saxophone
stop these young men from multiplying in dark corners
remove the powder from our faces
create festivals of flat noses
typhoons announcing royal compatriots of indigo
bottles full of flesh eating elixer to sprinkle around the
bankers create myths in little boxes on the rooftops
myths of perfume myths of skin glowing through the nocturne
myths of black coffee myths of shutters nailed shut suddenly
frightfully   opened
myths of mythical shaking bells
myths of asphyxiated gutters
myths of sanitized underwear
myths of underwear flapping in the wind like a tongue

this is our pleasure
to wake up shining a terrace full of erotic wind
a table with a newspaper open & ready to be devoured
a glass door holding more depth than our reflection
a hand on the knob abandoning barriers
an uncanny desire for socks in one piece

a room with walls of swinging smiles

Geoffrey Jacques

Dream Number 1

he ls the bearer of redemption
his eyes wear the sackcloth of osiris
he wears sourdough dresses
in the skull of satan
he drinks the dead meat of red beer
he has survived many nights of salted urine
he has tasted the female blood on his pillow
he is looking for the dream lite
he is looking for darkness
the toothless hag of the future
he chases rats from the room
and licks the wounds from old photographs
he licks the dew from the walls
armed with blankets and pills
he has rushed the five alarm fire of day
his mouth a century old scowl
he has fallen to his knees
repentant darkness
to swallow it whole
and let it gush from his pores
his grandmother whispers tantric
verse in his ear
his organs shudder
he dies the death
of many dreams
he pulls his eyelids
to his knees
and reaches to
touch himself
and finds
that he is
god

Ron Allen

Am I Who

who am i
scars on a junkie's arm
a rapist run rampant
out of society's neglect
the bastard son
of limp wrist proletariat soldiers
am i all there is
the sum total of one
am i the purple vomit of ethnic rain
the toe of unfilled condoms
the fiery face of beelzebub
the christ finally hung
for the sins of his mother
who am i
not that i am
anything else
the sum total of one
the wasted tissue of public urinals
am i the bottle of myriad labels
the mildew kisses of rabid dogs
the plasma of ninety cent wine
the bullshitter of pregnant words
who am i
not that i am
anything else
the whole total of one
who vagrant cultural imperialist
primal erection
cement and industrial wine
the laughing fist of chauvinism
the arc of yr vagina i am
the zionist eyes with
mediterranean bullets
god's tongue spitting

words through yr head
am i the flattened breasts
of my mother
who am i
not that i am
anything else
the whole total of one
am liars junkies thieves
am i
am i
metal teeth praying
to the pussy of love
the flourocarbon of dead flesh
demonic buck
oracle of the black tao
spitting seeds
into the anus of creation
am i who
who
the sum total of one
am i

Ron Allen

The Musician

A gaunt man
Carrying a battered saxophone case
Trudged down the grimy street
Bird memories
Bright against the Autumn sky
A soul aged in mellow crimson flames
Of cornbread sun and cottonflower moon
Trudged down the grimy street
Hearing the distant call of a trumpet
Visions of fingers gliding over ivory keys
To give love through his horn
Greeting red eyes
In the smoky haze
Bent by the weight
Of a thousand jimcrowed yesterdays
Passing moments
Regrets
Loomed silent like forgotten afternoons
Nodding in the ragged chair
Nights of love and violence
It was time
And a flood of notes cascaded from the horn
Life poured into creation

Michael Nance

Hope

(for Melanie)

Winter scrapes my heart
And bleeds it dry
If merely a warm smile
A caress
Can heal-
Why then
Oh spirit of warm spring
Does even love
Hang precariously
Like a limb
Broken by heavy snow?
We loved
And walked toward tomorrow
With arms entwined
Then from the depths of ourselves
Brought forth
A tiny human
Bathed in happy tears-
Of joy this time
And not the accursed other
That seemed to haunt us endlessly
But even in the gutted depths
Of emptiness
Amid the ashes
A flower blooms
And hope showers petals
Over the graves of our sorrows
A shoot bursts through
Green-eyed in the afternoon

                    Michael Nance

Azania

Black people
Do you hear
Your brothers groan
In the hellholes
Of South Africa
Pits dug in the earth
To feed gold and diamonds
To the greedy Boers?
Do you hear
The wailing of the hungry children —
Their playmates butchered by the jackbooted fiends?
Do you hear
The cries of the brave ones
Tortured on Robben Island
For standing up as men
Baking in the hot African sun
Getting only a stream of piss
In the face
When they ask for water?
Do you hear
The lamentations of the women
Starving in the sham Bantustans
Their men dragged off
To an horrendous fate?
Do you hear?

Michael Nance

The Deep Hat Boys

And the style
of the deep hat boys
expired while
the commodity of note
in the colonial marketplace
became the mysteries
of Karnak of the Khemt
Last night I dreamt
of my Borsalino being
sported by someone else
and after Antonio and Mussolini
the papal college chose
pharonic lids
like "zoot suits"
and florid point-toed shoes
the style of the deep hat boys
shouted a collective unconscious
grander than the grey
flannel archtype
so their style
like their syntax
reflected the collateral mode
a sympathetic magic
like the doll of the "vudun"
and the magic of the mysteries
brought baubles in the market
for the shaman
and riches for the trading
the post of the ether
so the deep hat shamans
languished in drunk tanks
or on base-bawl teams
while watching game shows
so the deep hat fell
into disrepute while

bauble merchants redefined
the gestalt and sold
the shamans wares
the artifact labors unconscious
to reexpress itself
as object which
is the style
of the deep hat boys

Faruq Z. Bey

Zelime

zie a moin semble fontainne,
dipi mo pli garde to.

-Creole Folk Song

Were it not for your eyes, Zelime,
Your green-grey eyes which pushed away
The dusty smoke of those terrible nights,
Which made little doors for me to enter
Beyond my weary, worrisome days, I would
Have forgotten the light that bonds us
One to another. You reached for me despite
Grave shadows of custom and law. I would
Have sworn against God and King to have that
Light. But you preferred our dangerous meetings
Near the Plaine amid the shouts and drums, the*
Swish and twirl of fierce dance for our stolen
Touches. And then you were gone. Each Sunday
I linger at the spot, grow old with thoughts
Of you, tire of the Bamboula, the rough Calinda.
Where are you now as the curfew booms? Where are
You now, as my heart grows dark?

*Congo Square or Place Congo — a public square in 18th and
19th century New Orleans where slaves were allowed to gather
for recreation.

Sybil Kein

56

Untitled I

So, I come back now
To the makeshift matchbox nest,
To greet you
Puzzled in your old age
At the depth of my injury
Sustained in the DMZ
Where you and my mother
Used to return daily,
With worms and sticks and mud.

You are puzzled
That it would take so long
For a wound to appear
Let alone to heal
Such unkind realizations come to me now.
For I have been through the places,
Where men make themselves,
Images apart from hearts
Eyes without tears
And hands made of bone only
The locker rooms
The barbershops

The open sewers we wade in
At the porno-pits
And yes, the factories
And like you

I have left my blood and shit in these places too
And eaten my brains out with fire
In exchange
And I come back now
to the nest shifting,
In the tall metal branches,
To forgive the dumbness,
Of our rage and confusion
Come with the gift of empty hands,
To cup your shoulders
And comfort the silence with a whisper
To say
I understand

                                        Kim Hunter

Untitled II

Imagine
That Charlie Parker had died
Playing
In the city
Of your choice
Before
You knew who he was
In reality
Would you have
Attended the pre corpse
Of a funky stone cold junky
Could you have struck up a conversation between sets
What would you have said:
"Oh...Uh...Bird, I think your wings are burning"

In this nation of images
Imagine
The city of your choice
Where the average child is nearly deaf
Where slum dwellers inject themselves
With perfume and fake gold
How could anyone know or care
That a human born with wings
In a storm of fire
Flew and blew heart away
While his wings burned

It seems a miracle that anyone cares
How he used that flame
In his

Brief
Def(t)
Spiral through the constellations
Oh yeah
He knew the route
His existentialist travel agent friends
Had put the consequences to him
Ripe and undeniable
And still and yet and even then

Would you have gone
So far above the ground
With a plastic saxophone
Knowing
What kind of motherfuckers
Were waiting for you
To return

Kim Hunter

After Mechanic Tuned the Engine,
It Ran Out of Key

Under the hood, I grabbed spark plug wire at
the boot and pulled it off. Slid a spark plug socket
over the head and turned to the left. You can snap
the ceramic insulator off no problem if you're careless.
I already cut myself shaving this morning.
Something wasn't right. "Shit," I growled.
Goddamn idiot gapped the plugs to 0.035 of an inch.
I'd really given 'em a piece of it at the garage.
    "Ya call that a tune-up? Look, Bud, think I'm
paying ya to screw off? We're talking sixty bucks a
shot here, fella. Sixty bucks. Christ!"
    Felt a hell of a lot better as I slammed down
the phone. I regapped to 0.06, torqued them to fifteen
foot-pounds and put on some makeup.

Teresa M. Tan

Untitled I

they laugh saying, "chinese, japanese, dirty knees"
it catches him by surprise he is american born
in detroit and what is more his patellar regions are immaculate
he can think of nothing to say. imamerikantu he yells after
them next time. they combine gleeful chant with protruding
dentition and a stretching of obicularis oculi to produce
the desired ethnic effect. his mother is white therefore
he is white his hair brown like hers. none of this matters to
them.
he gathers a hand of small geologic samples lying
about and imparts to them a trajectory with intent to cause
maximum discomfort. he wins a trip to the principal's office.

Teresa M. Tan

Untitled 2

one contemplates ambulation in day's diametric opposite,
the atmosphere
a discourse in optical silence punctuated with glimmers of
white
voice and monotonous yellow hum of the moon.
accompany digital interlock with disclosure
of tired features and vague digression on a lonely cardiac
chamber propelling me out
of mainstream. in the context of life, my creature is red
how can red compensate for quick desire coloring an outer
bank of personality
when the essential question remains that bomshell is bent
on pedagogical warfare.

Teresa M. Tan

Driving Through the Fog

Believe it or not,
there is another poem coming on,
another poem he says,
another poem;
and FLOC people
still fight the grower
and the union hall is emptied
and the beer was good
and the music was good
and worker's concept theatre was good
and your reading was good too.

And the farmworker
still sleeps in doubt,
and the doors
remain closed
for them;
and my father
whispers low
into my ear;
remember the hard times,
remember the gente,
remember nuestros raices,
remember to write
well of them;
and 3000
marines
are sent
to Honduras/ Nicaragua,
and;
believe it or not,
there is still

another
poem . . .
through the beer
and the loss
of leaving
the people
who don't have
the time
to write poems;
another poem
coming on
and yet
there is another,
coming
on,
another
poem . . . .

José L. Garza

"hackensack"
(for mary lou williams)

named for the new jersey town
across the river from manhattan,

scenic hackensack,
home of the rudy van gelder studios

where blue note & prestige
did most of their recording,

this tune was recorded as "rifftide'
by coleman hawkins in 1944

when monk was in his 52nd street band,
the changes were from "lady, be good"

but the concept was monk's & he got it
from an asch records session with hawk

& the great mary lou williams,
its true composer,

born in pittsburgh in 1910,
sweetheart of kansas city jazz in the 30s

with andy kirk & his twelve
clouds of joy orchestra,

resident of harlem in the 40s
an apartment in hamilton terrace

with a good piano
where the composers

& piano players came
to work out their charts,

a close friend of tadd dameron
& dizzy gillespie, mary lou knew bird

as a teenager in k.c.
& again in new york, chicago, harlem,

mary lou williams was a composer
of hundreds of tunes & major works

including "trumpet no end"
for the duke ellington orchestra,

"camel hop" & "roll em" for benny goodman,
"cloudy", "steppin' pretty," "walking

& swinging" & "froggy bottom"
or the twelve clouds of joy, & in 1946

she played her "zodiac suite"
with the new york philharmonic orchestra

in the first symphonic jazz concert
ever to be staged, mary lou williams

spanned the generations
from pre-swing jazz

to cecil taylor, & in the 40s
she was a champion of bebop

among the musicians of her generation:
"we were inseparable," she says, "monk,

bud powell & i. we were always
together,

every day,
for a long time." she also reveals

that many of her pieces
showed up under different names

on the records of other musicians, like
"little joe from chicago" as "blues

in the night," or "what's your story,
morning glory", as "black coffee,"

or "walking & swinging", which appeared
at least three times

under other titles, like "opus
caprice" by al haig, "symphony hall swing"

by sonny stitt, & "rhythm-a-ning"
by monk in 1957, by which time

ms. williams had abandoned
entertainment & the performing arts,

worked as a nurse & committed
her music to the church, writing

"mary lou's mass"
& many other original works

in the spiritual idiom.
she reminds us: "jazz

came out of the suffering
of the early black slaves; i think

it was born
in mississippi.

when i was seven years old,
i used to hide

under my great-grandparents' bed
& hear them talk about that,

how the slaves
created the music

& so forth. all of that music
is spiritual music. it's for human beings,

not for someone to walk around with an ego.
naturally the creators

could play it
with a better feel,

but it was created
for everybody to play."

John Sinclair

Passatempo

writing
nothing
in par-
ticular

for nobody
special

as often
as
possible

under
unimag
inable
circum
stances

for rea-
sons too
vague to

remember

tracking
sleep
like a

bloodhound

Paul Lichter

Images

1.
One student (white),
leading a class discussion
of *Native Son*
and running out of things to say,
asked, "How would you feel
if you encountered Bigger Thomas
on a dark street
late at night?"

Another student (black, astute)
countered: "How
would you know it was
Bigger Thomas?"

2.
I pictured him as muscular,
dull-eyed and dense, his sullen scowl,
skin color, maze of hair,
and criminal demeanor defining
my most horrendous nightmare.

How can I reconcile
that image
with this tender yellow
boy who could have been
my son?

                                    Naomi Long Madgett

(From *Octavia and Other Poems* by Naomi Long Madgett.
     Chicago: Third World Press, 1988)

South Africa Lives Here
(for Winnie Mandela)

South Africa lives in this house.

at your front door are boers
the uninvited marauders
come to take your song from you
come to take your money & your hope
at your front door are babies
            and bill collectors
            and blues singers
wailing out of tune

South Africa lives in this house.
in Detroit, New York, Houston,
the color lines and soup lines grow endless
as a horizon's reach, reaching
to touch those who tumble
from the flat edges of the world
as the hunger of isolation feeds on our bones
you will know Soweto
in the red zone lines
shanties crowded with dope & death
the odious crimes against itself
you will know Johannesburg
in a child selling his flesh on the streets,

the herding in the underpaid laborers
in Philly, El Salvador, Namibia
South Africa lives here—
on the plains of Nicaragua
the mountains of Chile
the rain forests of Zaire
all who know the ubiquity of its rivers
running thru parasitic veins
the packing in of trains with manufactured souls
South Africa lives in Brazil
        Angola   India
South Africa lives under the mask
of many governments & ideas & religions
forget the helpful
smiley face masks they wear
they are all the same tribe of monkeys
doing a tarzan dance in the trees
and stealing the blood of the mango
forget the whoredom of our leaders
lagging behind their mastuhs proud as house dogs
for their purina chow slice of life.

South Africa lives in this house.
in Chicago, Lagos, Port-Au-Prince
in the battered homes
        the battered lives
the broken metal that leaves a slither in the eye
and the terrible aching
you will know
in the sagging breasts & manless bed
        of her moans
South Africa lives here—
everywhere the winds of oppression
stir up the brown dust
everywhere defecated cowboys roam

you will know her as the soul mate
you hadn't dreamed of
yet knew right away
you will know her as your mother
who carries your hurt like a goatskin of water
South Africa lives in this house.
she is your mother.

this is her house
wherever we are
        and she knows it
        like she knows her name
                is Winnie
see her strut her freedom stuff
                on the front lines?

South Africa lives in this house.
this is her house
    and she knows it.

Nubia Kai

Revolution is Realism
(for Ibn)

we came together out of the same sadness,
i realize now, counting the times i've seen you weep
felt your caring pain in the wetness of your shirt,
the same one that gathered the moths
from the light & scent of sandlewood.
and just as a rose gives its beauty
out of a tangled root of horrors
i felt the anguish in the forest of your beard
giving so naturally
we think you are air or water
and everybody knows air and water
are dumb equations of molecules that don't hurt
yet, we know they hurt the most
cuz they feel the hapless battle
of humanity with invisible knights
the unchivalrous cutthroats of spirit
claiming the thrones of the ethers
— and who are we
to defeat the mother of the winds?
blowing a demon led coup d'état against the will
and wonderment of eclipsed mornings

to be a good man is crazy
who cares about roses in the jungle of the city?
they are soar spots
upsetting the equilibrium of war torn faces
scarred bad as a decapitated soldier
who stepped on a hand grenade
marred uprooted cut down
like the elms that once lived on

the block with us, then left the city
where we stand at the gravesites
of their shadows wishing there was shade
        or a passageway outta here.
how sad the hour that never moves
the hushed stillness of paralyzed veins
and the knowing heart that explodes
at the wall of sirens
how gloomy the landscape
with no center, no shrine
no flags of empowerment waving
over the burnt skeletons of capitalism
a menagerie of mangled minds
already captured and praying for death
rather than the slow agony of the ant hill.

so many times
we came to the edge of the otherside
knowing the death of revolution
was our own death
its resurrection our life
no utterances or chants of promise anywhere.

is it strange that
we could still love thru all this?
catching my hand on the tightrope
we come across, safe and grateful
we found each other
knowing God had his way this time
                why not again
                why not always.

                        Nubia Kai

The Crystal Globe I
(To Juan Emar, visionary of the Globe)

Only the green equatorial vulva
The blackhole of the divine emerald
Will give birth, will darken the transparent globe of my
dreams.
Dreams of emeralds! Baroque filigree!
Your blood up there, down there, your blood spilled among
voracious   abysses
Where submarines and other fishes, other miracles
Crossed the smoke cloud of the possible
The queen and the unicorn joined together under extravagant
    constellations
And the teeth of strange paradoxes
Beating, like widow's bones
Or of a prince's —the poor prince— down, up
In "the atrocious river of dust"*
A pair of little red shores, the magic and irate
Footware of innocents
With crazy, unshaken walking, everything
is confounded in the Globe that receives the tribute
Here diminished, here wet
Here drilled through, camouflaged
Here naked as "The girl who died in Paris"**

*A quotation from Peruvian poet César Vallejo
**Popular song of the twenties

Hernán Castellano-Girón

Translated from Spanish by William Little

Summer

You driving your car
that hot summer day
waving your skirt
above your own lap
making a breeze
one hand on the wheel
raising your skirt
higher and higher
there in the car
increasing the breeze
above your bare legs
then starting to laugh
waving it higher
laughing for joy
laughing for everyone
laughing and driving and
waving your skirt
higher and higher
wonderfully high

and I there beside you
O still as a weight
to know every move.

Lawrence Pike

Snoring

A sound from some dark place where membranes hide —
a snort, then a grating breathy rip,
a nasal Moby Dick that issues up
and jams the senses of his sleeping woman.
And he, dumb agent of all — the man
who hugs oblivion, who never knows
until he's told, who even then will cover
and deny, as when his sweetheart says
you made the whole house shake and he replies
what do you mean, I didn't hear a thing,
or maybe laughs sure sure, go plug your ears.

So what to do? There are no cures. Doctors
tell them separate beds. Such poor advice —
it takes all night to cozy into love.
Besides he sees the sneering surgeon's need
 to cut, to amputate the pimpled leg,
to bleed the common cold. And folks down home

try clothes-pins on the nose, but that fails too.
He says those clamps could make a nostrilled guy
look more like Harpo Marx or Dagwood Bumstead.
No princess wants a dunce between her sheets.
No woman wants to mock the man she holds.

Well then? We live with what we have. Now hear
our snorer giving in to sleep, to waves
of poppies cushioning his fall. How sweet
his breathing was in the first purr. But purrs
beget a drone and dronings turn to rumbles . . .
no, more as if a monster of the deep
has been there brooding, swallowing small fish
and swelling huge. Till rumbles swell to
roaring palates. So much noise! And now
milady's up and shouting *quiet, quiet!*
Wake up you goddam bastard! . . . . . .

But that's a risk we take when bedding down.
Things go bad if love is pierced by sound.

Lawrence Pike

Hamp and Marie

In schools i have read from classic books
seen honored art in museums
in chamber the music of old masters trained my ear

But at the feet of my father the literature of
a do-right life was explained
trotting and skipping behind daddy's path i
picked up lessons in honesty discipline courage
watching him work too hard for us i could understand the
art of love

My lovely mother comforted me countless times
counseled me drilled me skilled me in the subjects of
patience hope endurance grace faith
the spirituals that momma softly sang lulled me to sleep
a sweeter sound i have never heard

As a student i have learned that i don't know a lot
but the best of me came
from Hamp and Marie

Carolyn Burke

from: thiz singular voice

I
so take partz of me ashez
place them w/in the red earth
next to me motherz & fatherz spirit
in the black-bottom soil
of slavery'z door
take a part of me ashez
oh lord!
& place them on a plain tree trunk
so the winds will take me home
spilling a part
for the tear dropz on the red atlantik oceanz floor
don't forget to
hold ur headz high
w/eyez closed
as u look to afriiiiiii
                    kkkkkkkkaaaaaaaaaa

II
ur eyez go back to the boy
hiz mouth iz parted az if he'z abt to speak
hiz jacket iz open & hiz skinny chest iz bare
u see silver arrowz for ribz
glistening in the moon-day rizing
perhapz we'll play the bumper game w/him
perhapz we'll send them a copy-image of themselvez . . .

III
do explain to me mother why i had to leave thiz
place
thiz plantation called
united statez of north amerikka . . .
perhapz it iz not i that must leave
perhapz it'z the evil voice
the forked tongue freedom fighter
must be made to leave
on orbit-lezz craftz
where there iz no time motion
just empty holez of space

Ibn Pori Pitts

A Remembered Candle

Tears against my lover's cheeks
Enfold in each other's flesh
We weep

Our tears
Vibrant with pain
Seep into Sorrow's sleepless sea

And we
Enfolded and alone
Melt in grief
Drift softly into dream
And groan

A remembered candle
Lost within a distant room
Breathed out silently in smoke
And flown upon the wind

I whisper your name
I shiver

Rod Reinhart

The River
(from: Memorial of Flame)

Only the river sees me
He holds my eyes
Fathoms pass silent to the sea
Leaving me alone·

The sea gull skims the water
Soars to the Sun
The curve of her wing
Reflects my tears

I search for eyes
That glint of sympathy
The fleeting glance
To see my pain

People pass
The city passes
Eyes distant
Cold

Blind buildings and billboards stare
Whispers echo
"Diseased"

Only the river sees me
He holds my eyes

I sit alone
Silent fires
burn in my bones

Rod Reinhart

Winterblood

Crack Cocaine and chains of death
Bullets...struggling dying breath

Leave our children broken, bleeding
Shall they continue, still unheeding?

Walking down that road in silence
Dazed in drugs . . . bathed in violence

To the snow their blood is flowing,
'Till the snow is red and glowing

Mirror of mind, reject reflection
Into arms, inject infection

Lines of smoke, our children bending
Into ground, our tears descending

To your grave I touched a rose
A sob rose from my soul, and froze

Rod Reinhart

Penman's Song

scratch glick rub scrape
my pencil whispers music
it is a bow for my violin paper
chick chick cha cha rick a tick
shush choo
a drumstick switching a drumstick
claves or cricket's legs
screeching hushed rhythm
chug chug swish swish jug a jug
swoosh whoosh
hush
a song whispered
by the black lips of a puckered mouth sputtering
a black line swirling into designs
across rows even, waiting in line
standing straight, fluffing petticoats
colors speak lines sing sticks play
songs picture whispers move rhythms paint
sha na sha na sha na
chuck chuck chick chick babop a snap tick
shshshshshshshshshshsh

Angeline Kaimala

Indian Summer

sunlight on the yellow elm
and you and I just
know each other too well

mellow momentarily we may
be ready and fond
of one another but

listen keep the dark
faith of the season
kid leaves fall

by halloween we will
be being mean
to each other again

Mary Ann Cameron

Beats

You know
some devils
take to your street
in pairs

like romance and
self-pity

Mary Ann Cameron

The Vesper of Vietnam

Outside
faceless
cemeteries
of the pentagon
Maya enlists
the litany
of dead sons,
extinctly catalogued,
and chisels them
into a black, granite mirror.
a tribute triangled
inside the prism
of our own
peculiar misery
and the legacy
of dilemma—
of Vietnam.

tourists give awe
and ignorance
from monument
to monument
meandering thru
museums
where dead British
exhibit fox hunts
and anti-semitic
crucifixes,
while up
on the hill
quiet, brown caretakers
sweep footprints,

cook quiche
and listen
in
and out
of kitchens
to military visions
coded in luncheons
contracting alchemists
to mine uranium
from the Navaho Nation
to construct nuclear weapons
for outerspace.

Inside this tomb
of veteran signatures
survivors post letters
and faded, instamatic
pictures
reflected between
their ghosted shadows
and soldiers trapped
in black heavens.

Melba Joyce Boyd

Scenario in a Check Out Lane

I
"Why do we
aiways be waiting
in de longest line?
It seems
everytime
we's get up
to de register
it be breaking down.
It seems to me
dey should be openin' up
another express line
'cause
       shh---------------oot
dese here 4.8 million
be sayin dat
all de existing express lines
be fo dem.
Did you know
dey been having
more blue light pecials
den de whole world?"

            YEAH!

II
"Hey, don't you be closing
down dis here line!
My people
only got dis here
one item
and
we got a coupon.
Now, jist go--------on
and ring up
24.1 million people's freedom.
It's triple coupon day
and summer's a coming
almost everyday, now!"

Saundra Douglas

Name Poem I

(or No Sandy, Sandra, Cassandra, Cassaundra,
or variation thereof. . . My name is SAUNDRA)

"This child
is not going
to have a
nickname."

No shortening
Of herself.

"I don't want
you answering
to anything,
but the name
I gave you."

A rose
by any other
name
is a weed.

When my two vowels
go walking,
their relationship
creates
a new sound,
whole and full
with me.
Muffling my "u"
girdles my horizons
and/ you
ain't got

the right!
So, don't mangle
my name,
change
my definition,
rearrange
my concepts,
'cause
I'll tell
my momma . . . Euridyce Geraldine Hester Gay Douglas . . .
and/*she*
don't
eee---------ven
play.

                    Saundra Douglas

Snow Corn

(for our families who migrated north slightly before
"we," the children of the seventies were born)

We couldn't wait to come north
to these new carpeted places,
we are settled here in Inkster
just south of the big city.
These well worn sofa covers are
dingy from use
and TV light brightens the room.
The snow here is as hard to drive in
as the mud there was.
This Michigan cold chills me,
as I stumble sleepy to the factory /office.
My homage is payed to the not so
ancient african,
transported from the old country.
I sing praises to my granny
and the corn.
This child of the seventies is transformed
as this summer steams under
the green house effect.
         And yet we long for the lovemaking
under the displaced willow,
at the Isle.
Like down south,

my toes dug deep into the earth,
and it is pure
like you said it would be.
On mean days we are the walking rappers,
mumbling to ourselves as we perform
our tasks.
We fall off the wagon of brown
rice and teas.
And have whiskey,
when the smog is too bad
and too noisy to remember the poplar trees.
We sit in the basement playing soul
on the box,
defying pop music,
we dance in the bathroom.

                                   Leisia Duskin

For Tina Turner

Yes I know too
that I could have been queen
from the ancient river-yeah.
My cosmopolitan teas
imitate the ancient brew,
Tina yes you wildeyed sister girl.
Dancing legs under rockers,
I heard you sing the songgg-
telling me that you
might have been queen-yeah.
And I might have been too.
You are so fine,
the heavy brass bangle flashy
is the gold once worn proudly
by a nubian.
Your short leather skirt
mick jagger snatched off,
replaces the quiet contemplation
of the goddess.
Tina yes you,
The modern buddist reincarnation
of the wild wig craze.
Soul swinging grandma/ sister girl,
very old river-yes.
You never were as common
as the hometown watering hole.
You are timeless rivers
that never stop.

Leisia Duskin

Standoff

neither Malcolm's
nor King's philosophy
has been proven right . . .
or wrong.
only that it is
very dangerous
to talk race
loudly & eloquently
& to make any kind
of difference at all.

Larry Gabriel

Café au Lait

Piano
A violin solo with two violas?
High tea
Serenade to a symphony
A minor prelude to a fugue.

Counter cultural strangers
Sit at table
As pair.
It is discovered
That the girl came `a la carte.

Ménage `a Trois?
Three movements to a symphony
Arpreggios dart
We skirt the issue
That we part to a flat.

She says
"I can't go
I must have a
Café Au Lait
You know."

Detente/ she is a *dilettante.*
What started out as a cup of coffee
Grew into a four course meal.
She ordered bouillabaisse
It is a strange brew which brews.

The air is filled
with bouillabaisse, vichyssoise, and vermouth.
She says

"I may be a novice
But I have written a novel."
We cut the culinary calisthenics
And get down to the preliminaries.
The cheque arrives
As an affinity develops
Out of ambivalence.

Fait accompli!
No, coup de grâce!
She blows kisses in the wind
Amid parting glances/ as a souvenir
As a duo is left in place of a trio.

Keith Sterling

Nocturnal Emissions

Hot
Like slick saliva
Dried on breath
Staled
In summers heat.
I stir
Thirsting
For a taste of tenderness
A touch in the corner of night.
Heated
I am hungry
Full of the sweat
Of steam rhythms
With the night calling
As sole companion.

I am warm
As I bask with a fluid longing
Which ushers forth
And calls a cry
To the crevasses
Of my soul
With a grace
That springs relief
With a silent seed.
The emptiness, the loneliness
They come in cycles.
The coils of my body unfold
Wet, once again
And the night moans
As my mistress.

Keith Sterling

Desire and Free Trade

All day, this particular
Grey day, after Thanksgiving
We, carrying our car coats,
Haunted the malls;
Seeing so many pale, but never exact
Reflections or repercussions of ourselves
In the chrome, on glass
And in the ridged chic
of the mannequins
Until everything-even ourselves were reduced
Into a thick numbing stupor.

We ate our hot dogs and drank
A gigantic cherry-coke at the snack bar
Of a bright yellow linoleum fast food joint,
Then we took to the lanes again
Hoping to find something, anything.

Charles Gervin

Queen of the Molar Derby

Are you going sassoon? We
haven't yet reviewed
the marriage of tires
to the road.

Worth goes with notice
as vision is trick
root of visor width.

Back us into the dark
and monochromatic easy,
the weight of colorization
futures the hillsides
a shaky ripe neon.

But the real star is still
for windshield, waiting
for the improved face.
So lips stick to
the imported technical data,
and then you're free to wonder.

The enclosed will find
themselves serial pedestrians
imagining their polis
her ass on the seatcover.
The world a lover's commute
when car doors gently bump together.

The way highways
mile up to the next day.

                              Dennis Teichman

Rigor of Mortise

What turned the machine on was lack of
interest. Mechanical victory signs flashing
on the panels and you're left scratching your
head and rubbing your balls, thinking swine
woe me oh dee. She out produce me like a
fool.

Gender misrepresentation binds terms into
terminus, bracket bound to defend what's out
your mouth. "The minute I held her smooth
copper elbows, I knew I couldn't contain her
fractious horsepower."

Speaking in torques fills a glossary of
interpretations. Look around. Everyone's got
a girl act like shafts to the coupling.
Everyone has safety chains, remote starts,
linear shears, and off days spent being
wondered about. "Darling, you treat me like a
piece of steel. Explain that."

Don't you know. Try to visualize being snug
in a bosom of 52 tons. And then I handle.
Everything soft and cold, warm and hard,
vises, verses, and that which is essentially
braced to the wall. Still life with electric
motor.

A rule of thumb starts with eyes and travels
through the plant, blurring the window glass.
That's what you don't seem. Industry intends

its pound of instruction. Pause, flick.
Start, flick. Dream, flick. And gears worm
down deep into my heart.

Throwbacks to wartime dramas. Men and women
slapping each others backs. The camaraderie
extended to slapping names on presses. Gladys
and ol' Gus. Measurements prompted by love
from the back of the mind. "Scoot the ass
end over, just a cunt hair." "Six inches up,
six inches down." By the time you know enough
to snap out of it, what you got coming to you
is only outside, so you stay years and
enhance. Truth only screws up longing, sighs
the lone singer by the torch.

We sat around the sump pit till late in the
night, harmonizing our plight and swapping
blueprints. The collective nod off into a
sensuous background. Push the right
buttons, and steamy pipes await. These
mysteries of commerce made the rooms stuffy.
I made my exit along the routine air gauges
pointed towards the dark and atmospheric,
routed, casting a shadow rooted in place.

Dennis Teichman

Peace for Ali Muhammad

Peace without the pierce of torn flesh
Without the apathy of violence and shredded dreams
Peace
Without the lack of love
You know love, that which sits in the guts
And rots without peace
Peace   Billie singing   Coltrane   blowing
                 Mingus bowing
Peace without the dull knife jagger of self hate
Peace without the ragged tearing fear, badgering
and Annihilating beauty.
Peace without the cold stares that lie, but
Smiles like the truth
Peace without self eating anger
without the murder of vision
without the wild radiation of crushed innocence
Peace   Peace   Peace

Kaleema Hasan

Tenor Tears
(for Mark Anthony)

The night is always
rich with sounds hidden
from the day

A vacant lot
was transformed
marching to the sounds
of My Favorite Things

A solemn figure
playing a prayer
by the light
of the moon
captured in
in a naked bulb
in the rain

He drank deeply of
the dark through
his saxophone as
a communion cup
and blowing out of it
a harvest from
a cornucopia
bringing forth
that rain
to use as an accompaniment
rain drops as percussion
and the wind acting as
flutes whistling around corners
acting as strings
dying down to silence
and then building up again to a crescendo
to introduce the cymbals of thunder

and the rain played complex polyrhythmic sounds
layers upon layers of sounds
rain dropping on leaves, rain on roofs,
rain, rain, rain...

This sad sax man played a soliloquy
spoke of unfulfilled dreams
that only come semifulfilled when playing
he spoke of Coltrane, poetry and
new america populated with beautiful people

The rain cried for an encore
and tenor tears flowed
into the streets
into the night.

Willie Williams

Making Hate

It's what
they do best
in parked cars
and in turnstile
hotel rooms

Men bring
lust to
their hunk-of-meat
bodies and find
a new emptiness

Those who make
hate use
somebody else's
name and wish
they could use
somebody else's
body

When the weight of
the john makes
the bed springs
squeal they cry
for something
to
stick
in him

Irv Barat

Private Fire

From an upper storey I could see the city below—
the Museum with a few figures walking on its
sidewalks beneath sculptures towering
over the grass; and beyond the lights
of Christmas coming and below the district
where fantastic houses from the past crumble
housing the homeless, I could see the glass cylinders
of the Renaissance Center lording it over the river.
I couldn't see people wandering the empty
Sunday streets in the downtown that died
years ago, or the crack houses the police will raid
tonight, but I could see the lights
along the bridge webbed to Canada, and the suites
in the condominiums that disappear
as the sky descends from some night
we all await, anxious. If you've got a home
stay there; turn the heat up, draw the drapes
and let the news rock you gently till
daylight rolls back the curtains
on a ward where the sick tremble
and shiver.

I always thought people were easy
to alarm, that it took just a little to shake
them up, so I've been cautious. But tonight
seeing the city I recall
how easily we surrendered to one man's
private fire
as it burned out of control
taking the whole house till morning came
and the damage could be seen
beneath sunglasses my mother wore
against the bright faces of the neighborhood.

                                        Steven Schreiner

Passion Fruit

In the rubble of the Vernor's plant
newly demolished, men
pick through bricks, and the late
bright sunlight finds a hole
in the standing wall, a hole the size
of the world. The pink bricks
click and fall lanky into piles,
some for keeping tossed to the truck
where men stand in surplus store coats
beating their hands like boxes.
Two years ago Vernor's was an emblem
of the uniqueness of Detroit, Michigan,
its burn at the back of the throat.

Steven Schreiner

No. 125: Incident at the Tea Party

Well, He hardly ever hesitates,
    Only aptly, and with tea.
He could not never, ever deviate,
    He could not ever comfort me.

Well, He wishes
    (waxing-waning)
He wipes his tears
    For all to see.

"Where is my furlong furrow,
Boring burrow,
Catholic complex crisis?

Where do I price my patter,
    Chit or chatter,
Kneelling, pray to Isis?

What can I accomplish
    acting obstinate?
How can I absolve myself
    of this incident?
How will I ever get to Heaven,
Having hardly ever heard of it?"

And then he turns and-
    Damn this drama!
He bares his soul for all to see.
And, turning again,
    He is heading homeward
Having hardly touched his tea.

                        Rico Africa

Why Do Men Wear Earrings on One Ear?

Sepa yo!
Maybe por costumbre, maybe porqué es la moda
or they have made promesas, maybe for some vieja
for cosmetics or because some women love it
because they were on sale
because they are egocentric cabrons y buscan la atención
because la chica selling them was sooooo mamacita
and they could not refuse
maybe to tell you they are free, innovative, avant-garde
and liberated, maybe because of the full moon
because one earring is cheaper than two
maybe to keep the women guessing
and the men on their toes
maybe they are gay caballeros
maybe as a reminder de algo que no querian olvidar —
like the last time they had sex or to be sexy looking
maybe they are sexually confused
maybe to let *you* know they are very easily sexually aroused
maybe to separate themselves from los mas macho
maybe they are poets, writers
y la literatura is their thing!

Why do men wear earrings on one ear?
Sepa yo! Maybe baby. . .
they are reincarnated pirutos of yesteryears
maybe they lost the other one
maybe they are looking for someone good at cooking
maybe it makes them look like something is cooking
maybe to send signals — the left ear is right
and the right ear is wrong
maybe it depends on which coast you are on.

                                          Trinidad Sanchez

Chicano Warriors

On the edge
      this side of the new century
      this side of the year 2000
      this side of primavera
      con el canto del gallo
      the gods break barriers of sound
      through darkness
      of cosmic time - the stars
      bursting forth - exploding
      celebrating once again
      nuestra asendencia - our brownness
      la nobleza - royalty
      bronceando el futuro!
On the edge
      of worlds moving towards destruction
      pueblos en guerra
      sin espera - the gods renew our hope
      con nuevo esperanzas
      sending dos varones - twins - criaturas
      Andrew and Matthew
      to our Midst.
This double birth
      brings us to the center
      del arco iris
      con nuevo horizontes.
      Celebrando: sharing blessings
      bendiciones for our new
      CHICANO WARRIORS!
Este doble nacimiento
      brings us to the center celebrando:
      poeming, dancing, singing nuevo cantos
      telling his stories/her stories
      cuentos de los antepasados
      nuestra herencia,

so they will not be strangers
extranjeros in foreign lands.
Celebrando la fiesta at the center
celebrando el futuro!
we thank the gods
we praise them
for sending you to Vincent tu hermano
Vincent - father and Danielle their mother.
We thank the gods
we thank the heavens
for blessing us - la comunidad
la familia - raza noble y sencilla
with strong and new
CHICANO WARRIORS -
Andres y Mateo!

                                Trinidad Sanchez, Jr.

#56

Father Duffy, won't you pick me today
Wind chill is minus six
I'm 56th in line
& only have 3 Kools left
and everyone is hitting me up for a choke

Please give me a bag of bread & pinto beans
before my red nose turns blue
Father Duffy hurry
I'm the only white person in line
and I don't want to be seen on the evening news

Father Duffy
I'm cold
I've been here since noon
& I don't have anyplace to go

Open the church doors now pilgrim
the poor need the warmth
as much as the food.

Throw the grub out the window padre
& don't humiliate us anymore.
Father Duffy
You only have 55 bags of food
and I'm number 56

Father Duffy, Father Duffy,
I'm hungry....
Tonight I steal.

                                        Rob Rudnick

Collard Green Fields Forever

Have you ever seen
a crop of collards?
It is a vision of green magnificence.
Walking along an ordinary road in
Tuskegee one day,
I meandered upon a field
where some industrious hand
had sown the virile plant
as far as the eye could see.
Though the rows were disciplined,
the vigorous jade leaves emanated
an overwhelming energy.
Here was a natural power station
sustaining the faded and leaning
houses encircling it.
Spellbound on the field's periphery,
I remembered the Middle Passage,
and pictures of slave quarters at mealtime
whirled.

Collards and cornbread,
communion meal of
daily resurrection.

I ate the survival leaf as I stood at
the field's edge,
soaking its cure through pores and spirit.

Aneb Kgositsile

Calling All Brothers

*"And the male children were deaf to the pleas of the mothers,
and they couldn't see no men nowhere they had to respect..."*

Calling all brothers!
Calling all brothers!
Calling you out
from the hushed kingdoms
of corporate comfort;
calling you out
of your Mercedes and
your made-in America commitment.
Calling you out of
your cognac bottles.
Calling all my brothers
to break out of
your laid-off/unemployed blues,
break out of your videohypnosis;
calling all brothers, precious
as you are to your women,
cherished as you are by your sisters,
calling you out of your daze
of disgust with the family who sustains you--
your mothers, your sisters, your own brothers.

Calling you now
to *call off* your
"I ain't got no money, no job, no power"
dead-end trip. We see your anguish and
we understand.

Calling you now nevertheless
to the defense
of *your own life.*
Calling you to defend

your sons and daughters,
calling you to the defense of
humanity.

Dear Brothers; I'm calling you
to rise in the vacuum where
our African fathers used to stand
resolute against American madness.
I'm calling you to
take a position against children
with uzis and no daddies,
calling you to show the children
what uzis are for.

Calling you to a Great Reawakening
of African Fatherhood!
Calling you
to form the ranks of
your own army--
your own army--
to take the streets from the babies
so they can grow to manhood.
Calling you to dare
the babies to go on dealing drugs over
your dead body!

This is our war,
a war holier

than the Eagle
ever called you to fight.
This is our Vietnam, our South Africa
our Grenada, our Nicaragua,
in the streets of Motown, Philly, New York, LA--
on your block in our 'hood.

Calling you to dare
the monster death dealers who hustle the children
to face you down.

Calling all brothers,
crying for brothers,
moanin' for a brother,
dying for a brother.
Ain't no brothers nowhere?
Calling the makers of babies
to become their saviours.

Aneb Kgositsile

Untitled

Your hands sit and spin on the typewriter
while I wait my turn at ekeing out subjectivity.
At times I stare at your wrist, admiring the way your
thumb juts out at a right angle, your hands' philosophy
suggests linearity, or theories of calculus and geometry
so masculine and rational. I've been told that
we sexually desire from our loved ones their
embodied character. Seeing this in your hand at once
mystifies and satiates. I've been told that we seek
ourselves, those parts that we've disowned and are
attempting to reclaim.
Let me ask your hands. They can answer with a *caress*,
or when you remove your glasses, turn a page, or
eat with chopsticks.

Kim Nolte-Avalon

Trash & Shout

Through the good offices of the mayor a homeless
incinerator was adopted.
Chorus of roosters opens a play.
The orgasmic mother returns with the credits.
Like a song in a foreign language we hear the difference.
Trash elements beg the question about etymological chains.
As if they really.
You've got to have fresh air not to run for president.
As Catholics meet controversy a poetic idiom emerges.
The king's daughter reveals all.
What goes with it comes up again between us.
After highschool stains grow larger.
In each town there is commerce, acne, brightly lit restrooms.
Cheeseburger deluxe harbors power.
Imagine a medium-sized urban center making you cry.
We take our obscurity for granted.
Please do not open this envelope.
Chose a 13 year-old mudjahidine, heading for Eden.
Let him die for us, Allah Akbar accomplish a difficult task.
The poet was strapped by external influences, her midnight
shift.
A young girl makes a poster of a girl making a poster.
I am no longer a serious writer.
Am I the Morton Salt girl?
A Festival of Life is coming to town endangering the status
of truths whose fiction has been forgotten.
In the course of being inspected the trash was found wanting,
pushing the people under.
Night falls like success.
Everything begins on the margin.

Chris Tysh

The Day We Threw Out the Xmas Tree

there was ice in the alley was some shooting
the poppyseed cake all gone you came to the
door in your pleated skirt & white anklets
it was the day before anyone had time you
dispatched a bullet lodging illegally in my
shoulder squatting so to speak there on the top
floor of my body now shivering with shock
Holy Mother no it's not my leg someone please
call the cops somebody DO something! the day
we threw Julian wants to nurse furiously my
blood mixes with snow makes pink slush in the
hallway you're still standing in your camel
hair coat not in the least dishevelled though
not yet perfect posture is this being recorded
it occurs to me we're the last of our species
in arms I want two pints of fresh blood on the
street the good people of Pulaski watch police
ascend steps gingerly badges shining with cold
like tinsel the day we threw you came to the
whole picture unravels uniformly in this soap
there's only red tiny drops on the floor pressure
she said something apply pressure don't
break my heart sis anyhow where'd ya get that
piece of bad luck I put in two more rows where
the door opens & you stand clutching black
metal Jesus Fucking Christ they all said at
once the St. Florian nuns won't mind tonite
in their hearts so tender was the cake such
a fine lady

                                        Chris Tysh

Rutha Jean: White Friend of My Childhood

we watch mutual sunsets
seeking refuge in evening's
quiet siege
our differences suddenly
without breezes
we go confused
and wonder at the master
who deems us enemies

Hilda Vest

On a Hunger Strike

on a hunger strike not telling anyone about it
listening to the currents and rumbling inside
no time to tell anyone it was time
to consult the seer in the shack
on the outskirts of your senses
fire hiding in the shadows
someplace to warm your hands
he sits by the small fire
but you don't see him
you don't see the fire yet
stumbling through the glass
with aching hands and double vision
trying to pull your body off the wall
searching your car for a wrench
to unfasten the bars around you.
wake up before dawn
so they won't pick you up
shake it off walk out into the fog
find someplace open to get
a cup of coffee to go
back to your car.

Mick Vranich
Copyright © 1989

Untitled

Dreams reveal the source of our
    magic . . .
alchemical elements juxtapose
    silent tears,
wetting our minds — bespeaking
    a language of inversion . . .
the hour glass no longer keeps
    time,
archetypes dissolve into sure
    individual horror . . .
red tongues let fly the stingless
    bee,
murderous lilies dance a nude
    concerto . . .
        seize the alchera,
        walk the slumber,
        into the bosom of Isis
            fly . . .
        break bread with the witness,
        incise the stone of philosophy,
        and find the proper mouth
        to feed.

                Rudy Woods

Wild Kingdom
(for Milan Kundera)

This is your foreign correspondent,
Aristotle, for THE POETICS,
reporting live from the Mediterranean
where the skulls-and-bone of a few Egyptians
crown the tradeships of Her Majesty,
wave back and forth:
starfish—moons—Februaries.

To my right, our military advisor,
Hernando Cortez,
oversees operations at the Aztec/
Mexican border
where to the left of a stone no longer rising in water
a dove collects
its nest egg
upon the skeleton of a hummingbird.

To my left, our scribe-in-residence,
St. Nickle-and-Dime-'em-to-Debt,
scribbles furiously to a mortgaged future
where the last rites of man
and of-man
and delivered at the birth
of the lyric and gun.

Tyrone Williams

A Good Left Jab
(for Kim Hunter)

No meat for me, he
says to the waitress.

She seems to see, at
last, for the first

time, his t-shirt teems
animal agitprop, his

army surplus pants
aggress, his shoulderbag

bristles pamphlets, leaflets--
letters of intent.

Not the neighborhood. Not even this waitress.
He schools one, maybe two, workers.

Tyrone Williams

A Black Man Who Wants to Be
a White Woman

Doubts of a bride-to-be
a black man about to marry a career
a black man about to become a glorified housewife
secretary taxi driver cashier accountant stockbroker etc.
I understand the pre-nuptial agreement
a black man who wants to be a white woman

Thoughts of a black man
as a white woman will write well
as a white woman who will win
a place in my mistress' eyes are nothing
new under the sun that beats down upon the cursed brow
I understand the vehicles of these tenors
a black man about to become a white woman

Thoughts of a black man
who wants to be a white woman
who wants to write well
a typewriter with word processor ambitions
a typewriter that wants it all spelled out well in advance
a typewriter that wants to play around with the margins
themselves
I understand the warranty
a white woman who will turn back into a black man

Tyrone Williams

The Plagues
(for South African Boutique Women)

Dear
Socially Upright
Racially Uptight
South African White
Baasie Women sipping tea,
in the May
Rolling Stone
pressed linen boutiques:

How dare assume
you with straw hair
and bouffanted,
Blue eyes
the type
of superior stance
you do sitting
there, besmirked!

O palefaced
colonial BITCHES!

A spiked rusty finger
dirtcaked with the semen
of jackals inserted
in the foul slot
at the apex
of you cellulite
lined Rubenseque thighs
buried deeply, scratching
in the odors identical
to divine South African
black women
you so describe
yourself as above. . .

Hooked,
peeling the inside
of that blood-lined tunnel
would also
cause pain!
And the same lubricants
of fish coleur
would ooze therefrom
without GOLDEN DUST!
As it would
from all your SISTERS
white or OTHERWISE!

For such assumptions:
May your air skin
be ripped from your
flabby frame
with dull objects. . .
May your organs
be impregnated
with the shattered glass
fragments of the vile
teacups you hold
to your flat chest . . .
May your sagging breasts
be crushed
in a vise of red
hot iron hatred, until

exploding, your nipples
spew the blood and milk
of false heritage
at your fat feet
and from that ground
will grow
DEAD TREES. . .
May your Boer carcasses
by then stripped
of epidermis be burnt
so black they blot
your foul images
from the eyes of any further
cameras. . .

Removing you,
leaving only negative space
to be filled with truth,
violently.
                    Love,

                KARLA

                    Roberto Warren

Die Cut

Die cut not
like bleeding paper
gash groups bonding.

Die cut normal
together apart
from norms cut rotting
with replenishment
Of soul and
die cut positive energy.

Die cut singing
and dancing chants kissing
dying comrades dying
dried blood drying wet
Pored on the grounds of
chewed gum and grits
scraped from elsewhere,
hitchikers on old shoes
and spit.

Roberto Warren

Doors of Perception

how do masses
get converted
into liberated
energy?
is it really
in a flash of
enlightenment
or is that
just the end
of a long
process?

Allen Adkins

My Name

My name was shed in marriage — in keeping with tradition:
tyranny,
and betrayal.
But, even then,
I doubted the smile on my face,
and watched myself in disbelief.

My name, like my history is ignored,
the power of my legend withheld,
my record impugned — I prayed, as one in danger,
and searched my mother's eyes for understanding.

My name, like the body through which I was born,
the spirit in which I live,
and the thought which is my survival,
is denied.

But I assume myself,
confront my oppressors, and trust myself:
a Woman.

My name was lost in slavery:
in keeping with the nature of greed —
whose children are Cruelty,
Mendacity,
and Hatred.

And, even now,
my home is in doubt,
and I live in the wilderness
outside the land of justice.

My name, like my history is ignored,
the power of my legend withheld,

my record impugned.
The "Declaration of Independence" is betrayed—
but I honor the heroes within me,
and declare my own freedom.

My name, like the seed from which I was born,
the spirit in which I live,
and the thought which is my survival
is denied.

But I affirm my life,
claim my rights,
and believe in myself:
a Woman who is Black with the power of her people.

Mildred Hunt
Copyright © 1983

If You Don't Want My Love Poem

If you don't want my love poem,
I will cry,
wrap my arms around myself
and moan,
stay up late
watchin movies I don't see —
bleary eyed and swollen
for the mornin.

I won't answer when people talk to me —
I won't hear a word outside the blues.
I won't have an appetite,
leave my dinner on the plate all night,
stacked on the dish I left
the night before.

I'll wear bedclothes all weekend—
hearin every car roll down my street
(hopin it's you),
answerin the phone before it rings
(hopin it's you),
hangin up fast to clear the line
(in case it's you).

Comin out of love with you—
like bein in love with you—
will be a bitch.

Mildred Hunt
Copyright © 1983

Love Poem #2

From the eye of his organ
he proclaimed his love for her
so fiercely
she found herself reaching back
to a familiar age
she responded politely

he got loud

til she became more polite
but fiercely contorted
stretching from the decade before her
to the decade beyond
she was all things to him

louder came he

til her legs locked
her heart tight
up to the mind
round to the soul
down to the fingertips

loud again

til even her spit dried
she spoke
with a mouthful of choke
but found one scream
finally

one night
to bay
at a man in her moon

then she left the other
and his organ
for one

who only had eyes for her

Lolita Hernandez

Mike and Robin Must Love Each Other
(for Margo Perkins)

i lie in your lap as you comb my hair,
and we talk in little whispers
about mike tyson, and robin givens—
how much they probably love each other;

but their love was probably kidnapped
    by the media, like
the Lindburgh baby:
i imagine crowds of people downtown
watching the tv screens
in the window at woolworth's
for latest news
the FBI called in to search for what's been stolen
as if they themselves had not planned
this theft,
how when it's finally found
its little skull is crushed,
the flesh is eaten away (been dead awhile,
    the reporter says
and the coroner concludes
it must've been homicide with a blunt, blunt instrument.

as you spin some of my hair
between your finger and thumb
i can feel the rise and fall of your chest,
and think how mike might once have held robin
just like this, and she held him
just the way you hold me now.

Ray Waller
Ithaca, 3/5/89

Do You Know What It Means
to Miss Detroit?

1.
its cold there now, a november evening
an old man who remembers the myth
of employment,
drunk, graceful inside the prison of his days
leans back on narrow shins
head to the sky
like a stone on a hinge, something like a sigh
leaves his lips to find the air,
he weeps in front of an all night chicken shack

2.
no, aint no matter the slash, quick and nasty
cross the smooth flesh of the heart—
i shall, you shall love again, this,
this vicious city, yoursnevertheless.
listen: you'll love again,
even if just the love of the dancer,
the lover the dancer
who loves most what moves
(who loves the strong thigh
the slow calm flex
of ankle and toe
on saturday nights above mack avenue
on saturday nights yellow
in the ancient light of traffic

3.
nobody lives there.
letters return unopened,
unread, untouched.
when he calls the number
(that number that he knows)
someone lifts the other end,

says nothing,
the errant wail of a tiny siren
small and strange, is all he hears
before the click

4.
sitting here in NY he closes his eyes
he moves his mouth like a fish
and imagines a jumbo jet
a final approach —
runway #6 of Detroit Metro, blue and runny
thru the rainsplashed port. . .
the taut calves of stewardess
who in his mind
offers him one last pepsi;
in his mind there will be someone there
waiting to receive him, there will be someone
who will open to him, luggage and all.

                                        Ray Waller

The Mouth of the River of Eyes
The Delta

My age enters, squeezing by my eyes,
leaving cracked wands magically
sifting my skin;
Burning hard-won runes of laughter
and bittersweet smile
into my dusky flesh.

I sensuously shape
my Egyptian mouth,
letting the gathering age
press the torrenting wine
of my thoughts, my ideas, my attention.
I've learned to broach and savor
with these lips,
the aged mysteries
poured from a story's soul.

The Delta
in a soul's story,
whispered in an ancestral ode.
When I recall, then recite
the ancient story in my face,
We have a gathering of ancients.
They wait at the mouth of the River of Eyes,
waiting with a story to be told.

Jahra Michelle McKinney

5

On the road to paradise
above the silent sea
terraced earth
and Olive trees
visions and dreams
beneath fragrant leaves
below whispering leaves
I lay
where will I go
who have I been
here on Olympus
I cast out my sin
before purple evening dips
to black
and shadows dim
I sip the nectar
from the gourd
and chew these scraps of day
oil my spirit
sharpen my sword
for tomorrow's quest
and breathing deep
of perfumed night
I close my eyes
on the road to paradise

David M. Glicker

From Reminder on the Wind
(for Marilyn Marshall)

They found her in a vacant
house, barely discernable,
barely there at all. Out
of touch for long periods,
we were not shocked to find her
anonomously peering into us
from television news broadcasts.
We cry and the tears hurt
but do not help. They never
touched her when she needed
them to touch her. Never fell
into our pillows as the seasons
approached and passed.

We sit in our late tears
and cast stones. Complacent
people never throw stones you
know. Know this, cast stones
are passengers barely seen,
like reminders. We search
mirrors desperate for reasons
and discover wet reflections,

watch close the breath as it
forms on the glass, lingers
for a moment, then fades.

Life was a relentless sleep
rendered restless in a land
of barren glitter, her city.
No fame at the end of her
short stroll through this town.
No one remembers that some time
one life walked this street,
entered doors and wandered
through spaces habitually
filled with this and that.
She was a visitor
most days.

Stella L. Crews
3/16/86

Religious Instruction:
Book of Revelations

i remember
as a child in Chicago
not being allowed
to watch Mahalia Jackson on TV
and loving the music
so not understanding that prohibition,
i asked my mother,
why?
so she told me
how my father, when a boy of ten
in Texas
came home from school one day
to find his mother
    (a large woman, too)
being raped
by one of the white men she did laundry for
and he couldn't forget
how all she seemed able to do about it
was pray harder
and turn the other cheek.
so that was why he hated religion
    (in addition, of course, to that white man)
and why i
couldn't watch
Mahalia.
i received this news in silence
and transferred my allegiance to the blues.

Michele Gibbs

148

Laid Off

empty-handed
they hurry from habit
that assembly-line years
have geared them to
but now,
no job in sight
they fight
for dimes from passing strangers
hunt
for a piece of wood to whittle,
a body to beat
till it succumbs
taking on the shape
that mates us in defeat.
anything that comes in reach.
even yesterday's news, rolled up,
will do for battle.
something known, at least,
to mold and hold
to distinguish us from cattle.
for hands unused to rest
toil's test is easy
compared to this festering frustration
foisted on them by the factory's production freeze.
"Not much movin' now," says one
already missing a thumb
lost in happier days
when the line he worked would always run.
"If this was war
they'd send us home with more than this."

No lie.
some record that we fought and did not die;
a discharge with honor meritorious service

above and beyond all call —

something, minimally,
for the blankness of the wall we stare at now.
"We could even celebrate that kind of peace."

As it is, our blood, our sweat,
the pieces of ourselves that we exchanged for bread
mean nothing.

"Might as well be dead."

or, as another brother said,
"Just count us among the missing."

                                        Michele Gibbs

Sankai Juku:
Butoh Dancers of the Soul

We know that a show has a beginning and an end. A circle is drawn with a set of compasses, with a starting point and a finishing point. When the circle is complete, these two points become one and a form is created."

—Ushio Amagatusu,
Director/Creator of
Sankai Juku

looking thru the window
with the multitude of eyes
far from the masking of emotion
nude bodies break barriers
on the extreme perimeters of suffering
to expose transparent images.
slowly disturbances disappear
as eyes and I(s) wander
to the periphery of passion
their pale faces
persuading broken forms to feel
san (the mountain) feel
kai (sea) feel
the current of blue
as bodies frozen in tradition
evolve into gesture
no more transfixed faces
in the window
in the window
in the wind . . .

Schaarazetta Natalege

Memories of Mei
(for Mei-Mei Berssembrugge)

slant down sloe eyed
scandinavian doll mei
sings with incandescent birds
atop summits that move with the tide,
swims with fish souls and
collects random possessions, she
crochets precise poems,
photos the passion of landscapes, then
floats angular like a feather
in new mexican sunshine.

scandinavian sloe eyes
bathe with mirth in sparkling
oases of solitude as lizards bestow
her ancient gifts of mundane mysticism and
cacti flowers scent her with myrrh.
doll talks taboos with pretentious men,
dares sweep humor on politicos and
elicits eloquent echoes for children.

scandinavian china doll
hangs with midwest literati,
sips stroh's and also samples pizza

is she a poet? is she a princess?
is she the secret kept?
or maybe a fantasy?

Schaarazetta Natalege

Poets' Mission Statements

John Mason
To enlighten others . . . same as any self-proclaimed bard

Geoffrey Jacques
The best poems are autobiographies of the moment

Teresa Tan
I question and hopefully destabilize barriers

José Garza
Easing my way into your well-guarded misconceptions

Paul F. Lichter
More a CURSE, or an ENCHANTMENT than a set of predetermined intentions

Hernan Castellano-Giron
Everything goes to the memory, a great reservoir of everything

Lawrence Pike
A comic vision, poems and stories that entertain you on the edge

Angeline Kaimala
To communicate to people things of the spirit

Saundra Douglas
To make the time to create a poem in the midst of all this post 1984 fallout

Leisia Duskin
A record of the things of my life, witnessed and dreamed, that demand to be placed on paper

Larry Gabriel
There is no human life without art

Irv Barat
Writing: a vehicle to make sense out of the common experience

Steve Schreiner
Poetry is a harmony, to which I try to add my voice

Kim Nolte
I lose and find my life on a regular but unchartable basis

Hilda Vest
If I do not offer an alternative voice in this confusion, what will my grandchildren think?

Rudy Woods
I want to dance in . . . unconditional love

Jahra Michelle Mckinney
Poetry . . . a picture of where one's insides may be

David M. Glicker
A stylist and caretaker of language

Stella L. Crews
I paint it the way I would like to see it

Michele Gibbs
To unmask systematic barbarity and decay . . . to envision some other, more humane way

Sybil Kein
To Investigate the history of my ancestors, the Louisiana-French Creoles

About the Editors

Ron Allen and Stella Crews are committed to the promotion
of poetry as an art form and as a staple of the community.
Ron has been active in poetry circles for the past twenty years
as writer and, more recently, as director of Horizons In Poetry.
Stella's creativity is expressed through her keen sense of what
makes a poem worthy of survival. She is the author of two
books, <u>Thieves or the Laundromat Bandit</u> and <u>Salad In August.</u>
Broadside Press is grateful to these poets for their time
and talents.